West Sussex

Ben Perkins

COUNTRYSIDE BOOKS
NEWBURY BERKSHIRE

First Published 2008
© Ben Perkins, 2008

All rights reserved. No reproduction
permitted without the prior permission
of the publisher:

COUNTRYSIDE BOOKS
3 Catherine Road
Newbury, Berkshire

To view our complete range of books,
please visit us at
www.countrysidebooks.co.uk

ISBN 978 1 84674 066 4

*Cover picture of South Harting from Harting Down
was supplied by David Sellman*

Photographs by the author
Maps by CJWT Solutions

Designed by Peter Davies, Nautilus Design

Produced through MRM Associates Ltd, Reading
Typeset by CJWT Solutions, St Helens
Printed by Cambridge University Press

*All material for the manufacture of this book
was sourced from sustainable forests*

Contents

Location Map		4
Introduction		5

POCKET PUB WALKS

1	Fulking (4 miles)	7
2	Walderton (6 miles)	12
3	Milland (5 miles)	17
4	Lickfold (3¼ miles)	22
5	Graffham (5 miles)	27
6	Nutbourne (4 miles)	32
7	Sutton (5 miles)	37
8	Fittleworth (4 miles)	42
9	Ardingly (4¾ miles)	47
10	Staplefield (4½ miles)	52
11	The Haven (nr Billingshurst) (3 miles)	57
12	Nuthurst (3 miles)	62
13	Wineham (4 miles)	66
14	Slindon (5½ miles)	71
15	Binsted (4 miles)	76

Area map showing location of the walks

Introduction

West Sussex with its remarkably varied landscape, is generously provided with over 2,000 miles of rights-of-way as well as many opportunities for open access across heath and downland.

The chalk uplands of the South Downs are the most popular walking areas and are well represented in this book by five walks based on Graffham, Slindon, Sutton, Walderton and Fulking.

Less well known, but of comparable beauty, are the greensand hills in the northwest corner of the county, rising to the summit of Blackdown, the highest point in West Sussex. The exceptional quality of this area of the Western Weald is acknowledged by its inclusion in the designated South Downs Area of Outstanding Natural Beauty.

When planning the walks in this book, I was particularly keen to include the countryside of the Low Weald which offers fine walking across a patchwork of small woods and fields, often bordered with well-preserved tree-lined hedgerows, well exemplified on walks 11 and 12. The flat and relatively featureless coastal plain to the south of the Downs, where the rights-of-way are sparse, is represented by a level but very pleasant circuit from Binstead (walk 15) through attractive broad-leaved woodland, a feature which is common to almost every walk in the book and a reminder that West Sussex is one of the most heavily wooded counties in England.

West Sussex County Council operates an annual maintenance cycle on all their rights-of-way and claim that over 95% of them are in good order and easily usable. Though this is a statistic which must be taken with a little pinch of salt, most of the paths used on these walks are well-established and clearly signposted. However, some routes are relatively little used and you may encounter overgrown paths, particularly in late summer, and a stout stick might come in handy to beat down encroaching nettles and brambles. Also, where the footpaths double as bridleways, be prepared for mud underfoot during the winter months or after heavy rain.

The featured pubs, all walker-friendly, offer good, usually home-cooked food, often prepared from locally sourced ingredients, and most maintain a nice balance between the needs of the serious diner and the average walker who is likely to be looking for a pint of well-kept beer and a modest bar snack.

I have greatly enjoyed putting these walks together, reinforcing my belief that the only way to fully appreciate the riches of the English countryside is by exploring it on foot, always carrying an Explorer map and compass which I never leave behind, however familiar the territory. By following in my footsteps, similarly armed, I hope you are able to share this enjoyment.

Ben Perkins

Publisher's Note

We hope that you obtain considerable enjoyment from this book; great care has been taken in its preparation. Although at the time of publication all routes followed public rights of way or permitted paths, diversion orders can be made and permissions withdrawn.

We cannot, of course, be held responsible for such diversion orders and any inaccuracies in the text which result from these or any other changes to the routes nor any damage which might result from walkers trespassing on private property. We are anxious though that all details covering the walks are kept up to date and would therefore welcome information from readers which would be relevant to future editions.

The simple sketch maps that accompany the walks in this book are based on notes made by the author whilst checking out the routes on the ground. They are designed to show you how to reach the start, to point out the main features of the overall circuit, and they contain a progression of numbers that relate to the paragraphs of the text.

However, for the benefit of a proper map, we do recommend that you purchase the relevant Ordnance Survey sheet covering your walk. The Ordnance Survey maps are widely available, especially through booksellers and local newsagents.

1 **Fulking**

The Shepherd and Dog

Fulking is a perfect example of a so-called 'spring-line' village, one of many which were first established to make the most of the constant water supply which bubbles up where Downland chalk gives way to Wealden clay at the foot of the northern escarpment of the South Downs. The spring, which never dries up, even during severe drought, comes to the surface in the woods behind the pub. After a steep climb to the summit of the Downs, our walk follows the ridge up to a superb viewpoint on Edburton Hill. Dropping down to Edburton, another village on the spring-line, the return route follows an easy, level field path route back to the start.

West Sussex

Distance – 4 miles.

OS Explorer 122 Brighton and Hove, Lewes and Burgess Hill. GR 247114.
A walk along good downland tracks and field paths. One steep climb.

Starting Point The Shepherd and Dog at Fulking. There is room to park along the lane to the west of the pub.

How to get there *Fulking is accessible from either end of the underhill lane which runs along the foot of the Downs linking the A2037 Shoreham-to-Henfield road south of Small Dole with the A281 Pyecombe-to-Horsham road.*

THE PUB The **Shepherd and Dog** occupies a beautiful situation, tucked in at the foot of the steep scarp slope of the Downs. It dates from the 17th century and is now a free house. Although partly modernised, the low-beamed ceilings and inglenook fireplace have been carefully retained. The bar area opens on to a paved terrace and a delightful garden sloping up the hill behind the pub, next to a tumbling stream. Five real ales are available on hand pump, including Harvey's Sussex Bitter and a choice of guest beers, currently including two from the local Dark Star Brewery. As well as a substantial main menu, supplemented by regularly changed blackboard specials, the pub offers a good range of light meals such as jacket potatoes, hot ciabattas and freshly baked filled baguettes. Children and dogs are welcome.

Open from 11 am to 11 pm Monday to Saturday and 12 noon to 10.30 pm on Sunday. Food is served from 12 noon to 9.30 pm Monday to Saturday and from 12 noon to 9.30 pm on Sunday.
☎ *01273 857382*

Fulking Walk 1

From the back of the **Shepherd and Dog** car park, follow a signed path which climbs through scrub to a T-junction with another path where you should turn right and head for the Downs. Where the path comes out into the open at the start of the National Trust area of **Fulking Escarpment**, continue to climb along a fine terraced path, curving gently left.

On reaching a deeply rutted 'dual carriageway' chalk track, go straight ahead across it, still climbing steadily along a fine 'bostal' path. Towards the top of the hill go through a bridle gate and up to a waypost on the skyline where you should turn right, walk up to the top of the escarpment and turn right along a clear track, part of the **South Downs Way**.

After about 2/3 mile, a few yards after passing beneath power lines, where the South Downs Way veers slightly left, go ahead up to the summit of **Edburton Hill**, aiming for a small group of windblown trees. Walk across the summit earthworks, the remains of a Norman motte and bailey (ditch and mound)

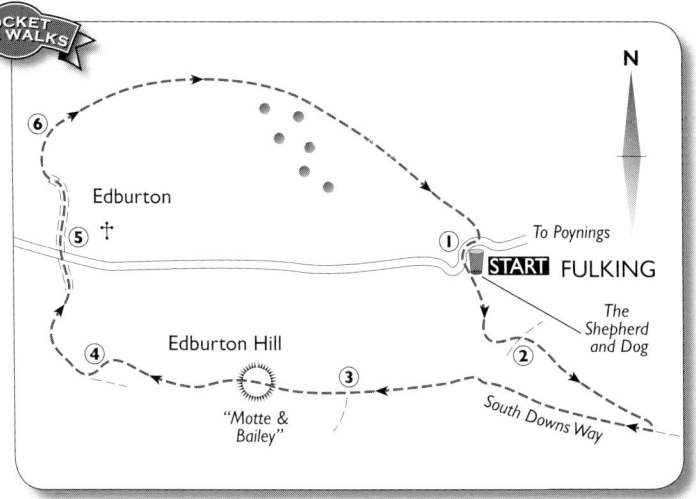

West Sussex

On the South Downs Way looking over Edburton

and continue along the lip of the scarp slope with a fence on your left.

[4] About 50 yards short of the point where the path rejoins the South Downs Way, turn right for 30 yards to a waypost where a yellow arrow points the way down the scarp slope using another superb terraced bostal which skirts round the head of a combe and finally descends steps to join a drive. Turn left out to join the underhill lane at **Edburton**.

[5] Turn left and, after a few yards, go right along the drive to **Brown's Meadow**. Just short of a light industrial area, fork left and, after a few yards, emerging into a field, turn right with a hedge on your right. In the field corner, cross a footbridge and turn right along a right field edge. In the next field corner follow a narrow path through scrub to another footbridge and keep to the right edge of the next field also to join an unmade track and turn left.

Fulking Walk 1

After a few yards, turn right along another hard track. In the field corner go ahead over a footbridge and continue with a hedge and ditch on your right. Go over another footbridge and forward with a wood on your right. At the corner of the wood, go right over a third footbridge and then half left, walking diagonally across the middle of two fields, separated by a driveway. At a second drive, go left over a concrete bridge. After a few more yards, bear half right on a stiled path across two fields and then along the left edge of a small village recreation area to join the lane, back at **Fulking**. Turn right back to the start.

Place of interest nearby

A few miles to the west and north of Fulking via the underhill lane and the A2037 is **Woods Mill**, headquarters of the Sussex Wildlife Trust with a 15-acre nature reserve, full of variety and interest. The reserve and a well laid out nature trail are open from Easter to October on Saturdays and Sundays, as well as Tuesday to Thursday during the school holidays.
☎ *01273 492630*

 2 **Walderton**

The Barley Mow

A **national nature reserve** protecting an ancient yew forest, a group of Bronze Age bell barrows and the delightful 13th-century church at Stoughton can all be found on, or close to, this varied downland walk. Starting from the tiny village of Walderton, it explores the rolling southern slopes of the Downs to the north of Chichester, offering a well-graded ascent to the 600 ft summit of Bow Hill, where you can enjoy a spectacular view southwards across the coastal plain to the spire of Chichester Cathedral and the Isle of Wight.

Walderton Walk 2

Distance – 6 miles.

OS Explorer 120 Chichester, South Harting and Selsey. GR 790106.
A fairly long but generally easy walk along good downland paths and tracks. Two steady climbs.

Starting Point The Barley Mow Inn at Walderton where you can use the car park if also patronising the pub. Alternatively, there is a useful car parking area next to the junction of the B2146 and the lane to the village about 200 yards from the pub.

How to get there Walderton is most easily accessible from the B2146 Emsworth-to-Harting road.

THE PUB The **Barley Mow**, built in 1740, was once part of a group of cottages incorporating a shop, alehouse and small brewery, though now only the picturesque village pub remains. The central bar is surrounded on three sides by comfortable seating areas, partly stone-floored and partly carpeted. A modest downland stream, the infant River Ems, runs at the end of the sheltered garden at the rear. The Barley Mow is a free house serving beers from the Ringwood Brewery, Fortyniner and Old Thumper as well as two other rotating guest ales. The varied food menu is supplemented by lunch-time specials and a full snack menu. Vegetarian alternatives such as parsnip and sweet potato bake are also on offer. Children and dogs are welcome.

Open from 11 am to 3 pm and 6 pm to 11 pm Monday to Saturday and from 12 noon to 10.30 pm on Sunday. Food is served from 12 noon to 2 pm and 6 pm to 9 pm daily.
☎ *02392 631321*

West Sussex

1. From the **Barley Mow**, turn left and walk out of the village, disregarding **Cooks Lane** to the left. Just after the last house on the right, turn right along a tree-lined track. After about 250 yards, at a '**Walderton Down**' Forestry Commission notice, fork left past a pole barrier and follow a clear chalk and flint track as it bears left and climbs steadily through woodland.

2. Towards the top of the hill, at a waypost, fork right on a narrower path, shortly bearing right between fences. Just past a ruined barn on your right, where a view opens out ahead across **Chichester Harbour**, turn left, still between fences, on a gently rising path across high open downland which finally levels out to enter woodland. Ignore the first signed path to the right. Follow the clear track as it emerges to follow the right-hand edge of woodland.

3. Ignoring a right fork, follow the track as it continues along the wood edge, soon turning squarely left. After 150 yards, turn right along a path which re-enters woodland. At a path junction,

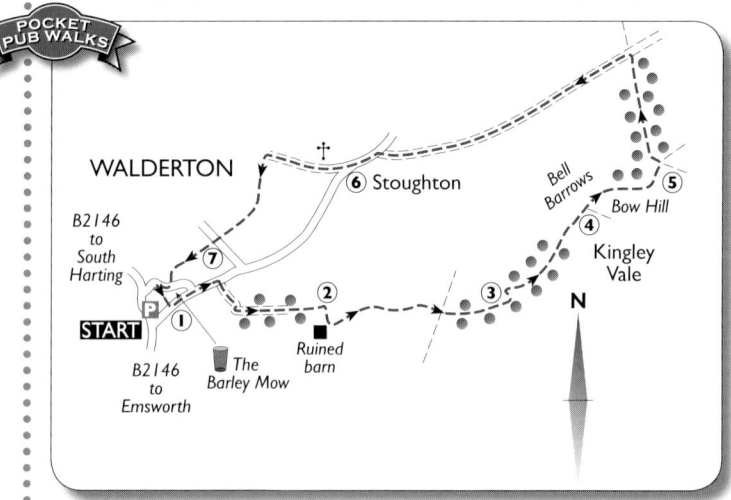

Walderton Walk 2

The River Ems at Stoughton

go ahead, passing to the right of a notice indicating that you are entering the **Kingley Vale National Nature Reserve**.

4. Leave the trees and go ahead across the open summit of **Bow Hill**, passing to the right of four Bronze Age bell barrows known as the **Devil's Humps**. Dropping down on your right is **Kingley Vale**, notable for its ancient yew forest. The view southwards across the coastal plain embraces **Chichester** with its prominent cathedral and, more distantly, **Portsmouth** and the **Isle of Wight**. Follow the main track, without change of direction, to re-enter woodland.

5. At a point where four bridleways converge and there is another nature reserve notice, turn left. Ignore a signed bridleway off to the left as the path begins to drop down. It then comes out into the open with a fine view to the left down the valley towards **Stoughton**, your next objective. Shortly, where a number of ways meet, turn left along a fenced path which drops downhill

West Sussex

and continues along the valley to join a lane where you should turn left into **Stoughton**, passing the **Hare and Hounds** pub on your right.

[6] Just short of the small village green, fork right, leaving the green on your left. After 100 yards, fork right along a track, signed as a bridleway, which starts immediately to the right of a telephone box and to the left of the access to **Stoughton church**, worth a short there-and-back detour. The track climbs steadily past some houses and then between banks. Just after the track levels out and begins to drop down, turn left at a waypost and head out across a large field, joining a right field edge and continuing across a second field to join a lane.

[7] The next path starts 5 yards to the right where you can resume your previous direction along a right field, subsequently swapping to the other side of the hedge. After another 100 yards turn left along an enclosed path out to a lane and turn right. Where the lane bends right, go left along an enclosed path which takes you through to another lane crossing the **River Ems** en route, little more than a stream at this point, close to its source. The pub is now a few yards to the left and the alternative parking area along the lane to the right.

Place of interest nearby

The ancient walled city of **Chichester**, a few miles to the east, was founded in Roman times and is of great historic interest. The four main streets forming the pedestrianised city centre meet at the 15th century gothic **Market Cross** and are lined by old buildings, many dating from the Georgian era. The cathedral, nearby, has a fine, slender 277 ft, 14th-century spire and an interior dating mainly from the 12th to 15th centuries.

3 Milland

The Rising Sun

This is a walk with a rather special goal, the little known but exceptional beauty spot of Older Hill, which provides a reminder of why this area of heath and woodland in northwest Sussex is already part of a designated Area of Outstanding Natural Beauty and should soon be included in the new South Downs National Park. The pleasant level field paths used in the early stages of the circuit do little to prepare the walker for the spectacular view southwards to the Downs which, after a long but well graded climb through woodland, is suddenly revealed from the 600 ft summit.

West Sussex

THE PUB

The **Rising Sun** is a large, relatively modern roadhouse-style pub, one of three in the area, built during the 1930s in anticipation of a planned trunk road which subsequently failed to materialise. It is a now a pleasant village pub, owned by Fuller's Brewery and run on a tenancy. The beers on hand pump are, as might be expected, Fuller's London Pride and Chiswick Bitter, supplemented by a regularly changed guest beer. The varied dishes on the high quality menu are all prepared from scratch using locally sourced ingredients and the puddings, too, are home-made. At lunchtime you can sample 'door-step' sandwiches, ploughman's or potato wedges with chilli mayonnaise.

Open from 12 noon to 3 pm and 5.30 pm to 11 pm Monday to Friday, from 12 noon to 11 pm on Saturday and from 12 noon to 10.30 pm on Sunday. Food is served from 12 noon to 3 pm and 6 pm to 10 pm Monday to Friday, 12 noon to 10.30 pm on Saturday and 1 pm to 5 pm on Sunday.
☎ *01428 741347*

Distance – 5 miles.

OS Explorer 133 Haslemere and Petersfield. GR 838270. A walk along field and woodland paths and quiet lanes. One long but steady climb.

Starting Point The Rising Sun Inn at Milland. You may park in the pub car park with permission. Alternatively there is plenty of roadside parking nearby.

How to get there *Milland can be approached either from the B2070 (previously the A3) at Hillbrow or Rake to the west or northwards via Woolbeding from the A272 west of Midhurst.*

Milland Walk 3

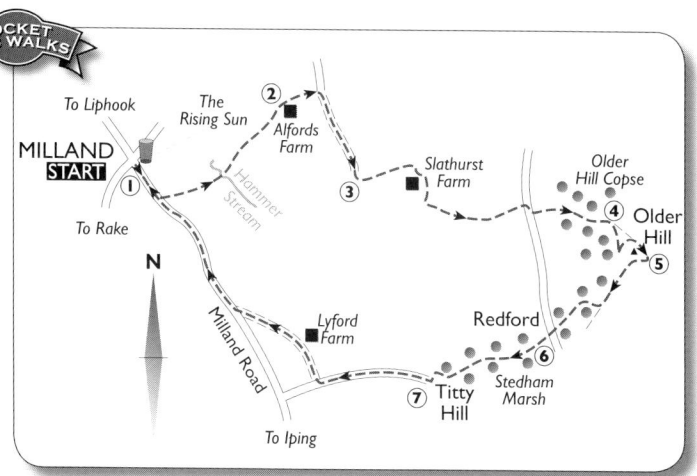

1. From the crossroads next to the **Rising Sun**, take the road signposted to **Iping**. After about 300 yards, turn left into the entrance to a house called **Myers** and immediately turn right over a stile. Cross a field, diverging at about 30 degrees from the fence on your left. Cross two stiles, passing to the right of a house and garden, and maintain direction on a stiled path through three fields. After passing to the right of a copse, cross two stiles in quick succession and head out across a field, aiming immediately to the left of the buildings at **Alfords Farm**.

2. Cross two more stiles, go left along a gravel drive for a few yards, then right on a path which skirts to the left of the farmhouse garden. Join the main drive from the farm but, after a few yards, go right over a stile to follow a path within a field, parallel to the drive. Walk round two sides of this field, down to a stile leading out to a lane. Turn right.

3. After about ¼ mile turn left, now on a wide unfenced track. At **Slathurst Farm**, follow the well-signed track as it meanders between the buildings and continues for ½ mile out to a lane,

West Sussex

The path on Older Hill

where you turn right. After 40 yards, go left over a stile and head out across a field to enter woodland over another stile in the top right corner. A path now climbs steadily through the wood. Go straight over two crossing paths.

4 At a three-armed sign, turn right with a low bank on your right, contouring along the wooded hillside. At another three-armed finger post, turn sharply back to the left on a path which soon climbs between banks. After about 150 yards fork right along an unsigned path which takes you up to the summit of **Older Hill**, a wonderful spot, offering expansive views southwards to the Downs across the thickly wooded weald.

5 Just past the trig point, turn right on a wide grassy path along the ridge to reach a second high point where there is a well placed seat. A few yards past the seat, fork right and shortly, right again on a path which drops steadily down a thinly wooded ridge.

Milland Walk 3

When opposite a large house on your left, where you have a choice of five signed routes, turn squarely right, dropping down through more woodland. At a tarmac drive turn left to follow it down to join a lane at **Redford**.

6) Your next path starts opposite. After a few yards, at a waypost, go straight ahead, ignoring forks to right and left. At a three-armed sign, turn right for a few yards on a path which winds round a fallen tree to reach a second fingerpost, where you should turn left, resuming your previous direction. At a signed T-junction, turn left, continuing through the patchy mixed woodland of **Stedham Marsh** to join a drive at **Titty Hill** where you turn left.

7) After 30 yards, fork right to follow the lane from this tiny hamlet. Disregard the first signed path to the right. After another ¼ mile, turn right over a stile beside a gate and go ahead on a stiled path along the left edge of three paddocks. Turn left to follow this drive out to **Milland Road** where you should turn right for ½ mile back to the start.

Place of interest nearby

The **Hollycombe Steam Collection** can be found about 3 miles to the north and east of Milland and is a remarkable assembly of working steam-powered machines, including a complete Edwardian fairground. The inclusive entrance fee allows you to sample all the rides including three steam trains and a traction engine. Open from April to October.
☎ *01428 724900*

4 Lickfold

The Lickfold Inn

The suffix **'fold'**, derived from Old English, is common to several place-names in the heavily wooded areas of north-west Sussex and Surrey, suggesting that such settlements were first established in areas cleared from the ancient Wealden forest. Starting across fields in the river valley formed by one of the main tributary streams of the River Rother, our walk then turns to enter an area of mixed woodland on the lower slopes

Lickfold Walk 4

of Bexleyhill with occasional views to the wooded heights of Blackdown, the highest point in Sussex, only a few miles away to the north. Although following generally dry and well established paths, part of the area may be liable to flooding after heavy rain.

THE PUB The **Lickfold Inn** is housed in an attractive listed building, dating from 1640 and fronted in timber and herringbone-patterned brick. The interior is equally attractive and unspoilt, and features red-brick floors and a massive inglenook fireplace. The beers on hand pump are Harvey's Sussex Bitter and TEA (Traditional English Ale) from the Hogs Back Brewery in Surrey. This is very much a dining pub, featuring a distinguished 'haute cuisine' menu, supplemented at lunch-time on weekdays with regularly changed and equally distinguished 'Light Bites'. (As this book goes to press, a change of management has been announced. The above details may therefore differ.)

Distance – 3¼ miles.

OS Explorer 133 Haslemere and Petersfield. GR 926263. An easy walk on field and woodland paths with only minor ups and downs, partly along heavily ridden and potentially muddy bridleways.

Starting Point The Lickfold Inn at Lickfold. Patrons may use the car park with permission. Roadside parking is possible in several places nearby.

How to get there *Lickfold, a small and undefined settlement spread out along a minor road, is best approached from the south. Leave the A272 at Halfway Bridge, midway between Petworth and Midhurst to follow an unclassified road northwards, passing through Lodsworth before dropping down to Lickfold Bridge next to the pub.*

West Sussex

Open from 11 am to 2.30 pm and 6 pm to 11 pm Tuesday to Saturday and from 12 noon to 3.30 pm on Sunday. Food is served from 12 noon to 2.30 pm Tuesday to Sunday and 7 pm to 9.30 pm Tuesday to Saturday. The pub is closed on Sunday evening and Monday.
☎ *01798 861285*

1 From the road junction next to the **Lickfold Inn**, start the walk along the road signposted to **Haslemere** and **Lurgashall**. After only 10 yards, turn right up a steep bank, walk along a short fenced path to a stile and go ahead, keeping to the left edge of three fields. A few yards beyond a stream crossing, side-step to the left through a gate and resume your previous direction to follow the right edge of two more fields.

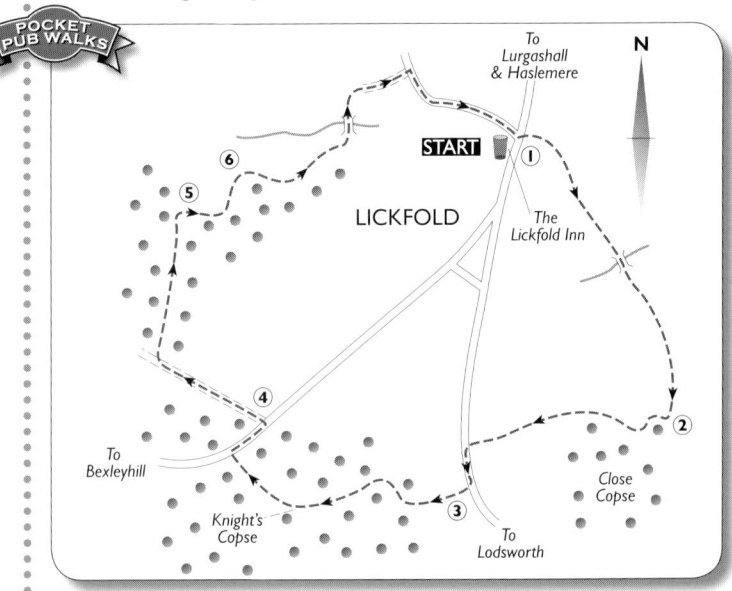

Lickfold Walk 4

Walking through Knight's Copse

Just short of the second field corner, turn right over a plank bridge and stile and follow a left field edge as it bends left and subsequently right with a wood, **Close Copse**, on your left. At the corner of the wood, go left over a stile and plank bridge and bear half right across a field, aiming for the prominent wireless mast on **Bexleyhill**. Go over a stile in a post and rail crossing fence and continue across the next field, joining a left-hand hedge and following it out to a lane where you turn left.

After about 100 yards, turn right along a wide dirt track. Just short of a high wooden gate to a house, turn right along a heavily ridden path and, after 10 yards, go left along a wide woodland path. At a T-junction, turn left and, after a little over 100 yards, fork right, still along a spacious woodland path. Shortly, ignoring a right fork, go ahead through old unharvested coppiced woodland, **Knight's Copse**. Continue to a lane and turn right.

West Sussex

[4] After less than 100 yards, turn left along the drive to a house called **Overnoons**. After a few yards, fork right along a path which runs between banks, parallel and immediately to the right of the drive. After 300 yards, just after passing through a shallow dip, turn right, still on a path between banks.

[5] After about ¼ mile, where the wood on your right comes to an end, turn right at a waypost and go ahead along the right edge of a field carved out of the woodland, where you get a fine view to the left towards the wooded heights of **Black Down**, the highest point in Sussex. In the field corner, go forward into the wood and immediately turn left along a wide track.

[6] After 100 yards or so, at a waypost, turn right up a bank and along a narrower woodland path. After a while, descend to cross a stream and turn left, soon with a wider stream, one of the main tributary feeders of the **River Rother**, nearby on your left. Disregard two signed paths to the right and cross the stream using an old stone-built bridge. The path rises to a T-junction with a wide track where you turn right. Follow this track out to a lane and turn right for about 400 yards back to the start.

Place of interest nearby

Petworth House and Park are within easy reach to the south and east via the A272. The magnificent 17th century mansion, owned by the National Trust, is set in a large deer park landscaped by 'Capability' Brown. The interior is notable for carvings by Grinling Gibbons and a large and distinguished collection of paintings. The park is open daily and the house is open from March to October, though not every day.
☎ 01798 343929

5 Graffham

The White Horse

From the unspoilt village of Graffham at the foot of the Downs, this walk follows a steep but well graded path up the heavily wooded escarpment to reach the ridge within a short distance of the highest point on the Sussex Downs at Crown Tegleaze. A pleasant level summit walk then passes between areas where the prevailing trees and scrub are being cleared, the aim being to restore much of the area to species-rich chalk grass downland. The views from the high ground are limited by trees but improve during the descent through partially thinned woodland.

West Sussex

Distance – 5 miles.

OS Explorer 121 Arundel and Pulborough. GR 926177.
A walk through woods and fields, using good paths and firm well-drained downland tracks. One long steady climb.

Starting Point The White Horse at Graffham where you are welcome to use the large car park while on the walk, if also patronising the pub. Alternative roadside parking near the pub.

How to get there *From the A285 Petworth-to-Chichester road about 2½ miles south of Petworth, head westwards along a lane, following signs to Graffham. Soon after passing another pub, the Foresters, turn right to find the White Horse on the edge of the village.*

THE PUB The **White Horse** is beautifully situated on slightly raised ground with a conservatory dining area and garden facing southwards towards the Downs. It is a free house offering a wide choice of good beers, including Ruddles County, Morland Old Speckled Hen, Greene King IPA and two other regularly changed guest ales on hand pump. The food menu is an interesting one, embracing pub favourites and some less usual dishes such as bacon roly-poly with parsley sauce or chicken stilton crumble as well as a 'Chef's Special' and a vegetable brie bake for vegetarians. Filled baguettes and jacket potatoes are also available.

Open from 11 am to 3 pm and 6 pm to 11 pm Monday to Friday, 11 am to 11 pm on Saturday and 12 noon to 11 pm on Sunday. Food is served from 12 noon to 2 pm and 6 pm to 9 pm Monday to Friday and from 12 noon to 2.30 pm and 6 pm to 9 pm at weekends. ☎ *01798 867331*

Graffham Walk 5

From the **White Horse**, turn right along the road. At a road junction turn left. Just past the well maintained village war memorial area on your right, go right into the start of a drive and immediately right again through a wooden kissing gate. Now head for the Downs, following a well-trodden path across a field and on along a wide grassy strip. Beyond staggered railings, go ahead, not along the obvious track but on a narrower path which skirts to the right of buildings at **Calloways**. Go forward along a gravel drive to join a lane opposite **Graffham church** and turn left.

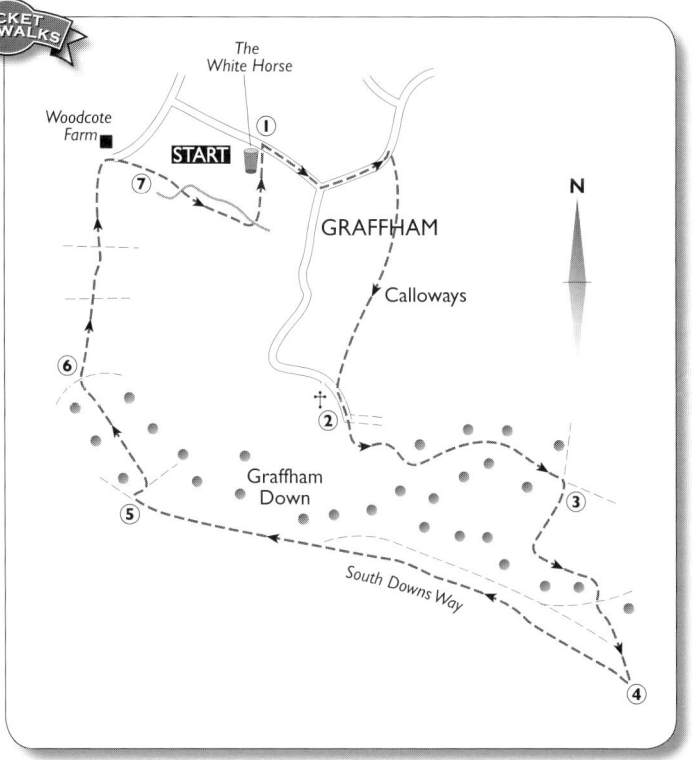

West Sussex

2 Where the lane bears left to become the drive to **Seaford College**, go ahead along a track which soon bears left, climbing gently near the foot of the Downs. On reaching a notice 'No motor vehicles beyond this point', turn left along a track which follows an undulating course near the foot of a steep wooded slope. Disregard several paths scarred by motor vehicles as well as the first signed path off to the right, with a blue waymark.

3 After another 300 yards, fork right on a public footpath marked with a yellow arrow, which climbs steadily. Go straight over a wide crossing path. Towards the top of the hill, ignore a left fork. After a few more yards, where the path comes out into the open, go ahead across an arable field without change of direction, aiming for a finger post where you can join a hard track.

4 Turn right along this track, now on the **South Downs Way**, which you can follow for more than 1 mile, ignoring all side paths. Where the arable field on your right comes to an end, keep straight on, passing to the right of an area of downland currently being restored to traditional chalk downland by the **Graffham Wood Trust**.

5 After another ¼ mile, after passing another cleared area to the right of the path, turn sharply right along a signed crossing track. After 100 yards, turn left along a narrower path which drops obliquely down the wooded downland escarpment, with intermittent views northwards towards **Graffham** and into the **Weald**. Go straight over a crossing track and, at a second crossing track, go right for 10 yards, then left. After 60 yards, go right to leave the wood over a stile.

6 Now follow a path which takes a relatively straight course through several fields and then a track to reach **Woodcote Farm**, ignoring two crossing paths en route. Walk between the farm buildings and turn right to follow the lane from the farm.

Graffham Walk 5

Shortly, where the lane bends left, fork right over a stile to the right of a gate and walk along a right field edge with a house and garden on your right.

At the corner of the garden go right and, after a few yards, left to follow a line of trees between two fields. At the other side of these fields bear right down to cross a stream and up to a stile. Now bear left along a left field edge until, after 250 yards, you can go left over a stile. Walk back over the stream to a stile, cross a field corner to another stile and then follow a left field edge out to the lane next to the pub.

Place of interest nearby

Coultershaw Beam Pump stands beside the A285 at the river crossing about 1 mile south of Petworth. It was installed in 1782 to pump water from the River Rother to Petworth and the machinery has recently been restored to working order by a local Industrial Archaeology group. It is open to view between 11 am and 5 pm on the first and third Sundays of the month between April and September.

POCKET PUB WALKS

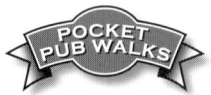

6 Nutbourne

The Rising Sun

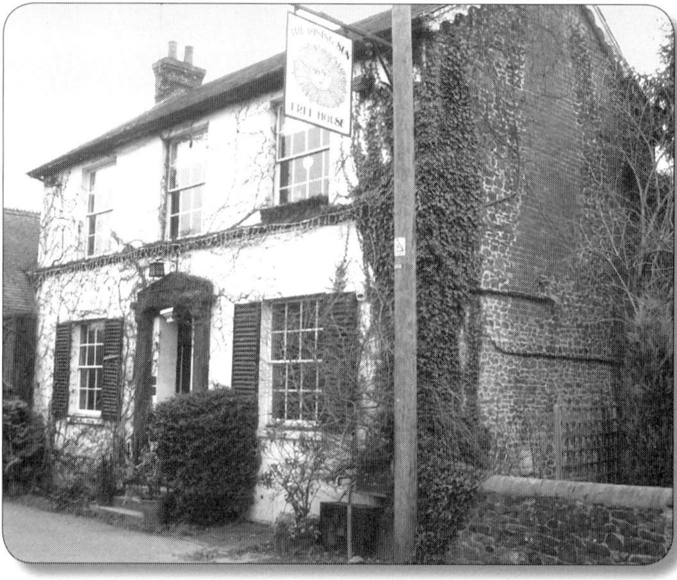

From the small village of Nutbourne, this varied walk explores a gently undulating landscape, once rich farmland but now partly diversified into vineyard and golf course as well as some new tree planting. It follows field paths and several trackways, probably of ancient origin, often running between high sandstone banks. The latter part of the walk rises to high ground and offers a wide panoramic view southwards to the ridge of the South Downs.

Nutbourne Walk 6

Distance – 4 miles.

OS Explorer 121 Arundel and Pulborough. GR 074187.
A walk along field paths and hedged trackways. A few ups and downs, none long or severe. Be prepared for mud underfoot on the bridleway sections.

Starting Point The Rising Sun at Nutbourne. Roadside parking is possible in several places along the village street in the vicinity of the pub.

How to get there *Nutbourne is signposted from the A283 about ½ mile east of Pulborough. Take the first left along Nutbourne Road to reach the village.*

THE PUB

The **Rising Sun** is that increasingly rare establishment, a completely unspoilt village 'local', full of character. The spacious main bar has scrubbed wooden floors and tables as well as an open fire and is complemented by a saloon, dining area and children's room at the rear of the pub. It is a free house in private ownership, serving Fuller's London Pride and a choice of three regularly changed guest beers. The main menu offers traditional 'pub grub' such as home-made pies, and also burgers made from unusual ingredients such as Cajun chicken and Moroccan lamb. The lunchtime menu includes sandwiches, jacket potatoes and ploughman's.

Open from 11 am to 3 pm and 6 pm to 11 pm Monday to Saturday and from 12 noon to 3 pm and 7 pm to 10.30 pm on Sunday. Food is served from 12 noon to 2 pm and 7 pm to 9.30 pm daily (9 pm on Sunday).
☎ *01798 812191*

West Sussex

1. From the **Rising Sun** turn left along the village street. After 100 yards, just past **Manor Farm House** on your right, turn right along a lane. After 60 yards, fork right and shortly, where the metalled lane ends, go straight ahead, ignoring a right fork. A gravel track runs between high banks at first. Just past an old mill pond on your left, turn right along a dirt track which soon bears left between fields of grape vines and then along the left edge of newly planted **Stuart's Wood**, which is open to the public. A gated path continues along the left edge of two paddocks and then past a house and garden to join a lane.

2. Climb the steps opposite and continue along a right field edge, now on part of the newly created **West Sussex Literary Trail**. In the field corner cross a culvert and stile and go ahead with a hedge on your left at first, then straight out across a golf course. After about 150 yards, at a finger post, go left along a

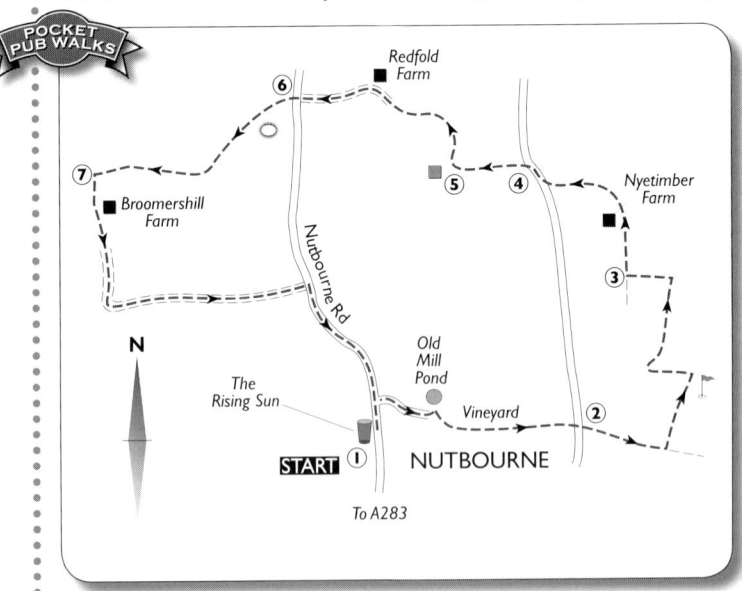

Nutbourne Walk 6

The view from point 2 of the walk

well trodden signed bridleway. At a second post, turn squarely left, still along the bridleway. At the bottom of a slope, turn right, continuing with the bridleway as it bears left and climbs between banks.

At a T-junction with a hard-based access track turn right. At **Nyetimber Farm** go straight ahead, ignoring a crossing footpath, now on a narrower path between banks which you can follow out to a lane. Turn right.

After 130 yards, go left over a stile and forward along a right-hand field edge. Go over a stile to the left of a brick cattle shelter and, after a few yards, bear right through a young tree plantation and along a right field edge, following it round to the right. Go through a gateway and, after 60 yards, go left over a stile and down across grass to join a drive over a second stile and turn left.

West Sussex

5. A few yards short of buildings fork right to a stile and cross a field, walking parallel to a right-hand field edge to find the next stile and then bear half left up across pasture, aiming to pass to the left and below the farm buildings at **Redfold Farm**. Join and follow the drive from the farm out to a lane.

6. Cross the lane, go over a stile at the top of the bank opposite and head half left across high ground with a fine view southwards to the distant ridge of the **Downs**. Continue across the next field to go through a gate next to a prominent fir tree and then bear right along a right field edge. In the next field corner go over a stile, veer right for a few yards to a second stile and then follow a left field edge.

7. In the next field corner, cross a stile beside a gate and turn left for a few yards to join and go forward along a concrete drive, following it as it skirts to the right of the large house at **Broomershill Farm**. Ignoring a signed path off to the right, continue past farm outbuildings and southwards on a track between fence and hedge, following it as it bends left and continues for ½ mile or so out to a lane. Turn right for a similar distance back to the start.

Place of interest nearby

About 3 miles to the south of Pulborough and Nutbourne along the A283 is **Parham House**, an exceptional Elizabethan mansion, dating from 1577 and surrounded by a 300-acre deer park. The house and garden are open to the public from Easter Sunday to 30 September on Wednesday, Thursday, Sunday and Bank Holiday Mondays, also Tuesday and Friday in August.

7 Sutton

The White Horse

The unspoilt village of Sutton lies well off the beaten track at the foot of, and half enclosed by, well wooded downland. Our walk starts out along the gently undulating foothills of the Downs, passing the hamlet of Barlavington, little more than a farm and a handful of cottages around a small and charming 13th century church. After a steady climb up through Duncton Hanger and a traverse southwards across more open ground, the return route uses an ancient trackway across the shoulder of Barlavington Down, descending as a sunken hollow-way through more woodland.

The **White Horse**, built as an inn 150 years ago, has had a chequered recent history. Closed for a short period, it is now flourishing once more, owned by Enterprise Inns

West Sussex

> **Distance** – 5 miles.
>
> **OS Explorer** 121 Arundel and Pulborough. (GR 979152).
> A fairly hilly walk, all along good downland paths and tracks, reasonably dry underfoot in all seasons.
>
> **Starting Point** The White Horse Inn at Sutton. There is room to park beside the lane to the north of the pub.

How to get there *The village can only be reached along narrow winding lanes. The best approach is from the A26 just south of Watersfield and Coldwaltham. Turn into the B2128 and after a few yards, go left along a lane, following signs to Bignor at first, then Sutton.*

and managed under a lease. The interior, although extensively renovated, retains the traditional division between wood-floored public bar and carpeted saloon. A dining extension has been constructed from an old wine cellar and there is a well sheltered patio and a secluded garden. Three beers are always on offer, currently Harvey's Sussex Ale, Fuller's London Pride and Young's Bitter. The food menu is an extensive one with some novel dishes such as Highland chicken stuffed with haggis. Sandwiches are available at lunchtime. Children and dogs are equally welcome.

Open from 11 am to 2.30 pm and 6 pm to 10.30 pm Monday to Wednesday, 11 am to 3 pm and 6 pm to 11 pm Thursday to Saturday, and from 12 noon to 4 pm on Sunday (closed Sunday evening). Food is served from 12 noon to 2 pm and 6 pm to 9 pm Monday to Friday, 12 noon to 2.30 pm and 6 pm to 9 pm on Saturday and 12 noon to 2.30 pm on Sunday.
☎ *01798 869221*

Sutton Walk 7

From the road junction next to the **White Horse**, follow the main street through the village, signposted to **Petworth**. A few yards past **Sutton parish church** on your left, go left along a drive. Where the drive ends at the gateway to a house called **Potcroft**, go ahead along a narrow path. At a T-junction with another path, turn right with a wood on your right, then walk down through the wood to a stream crossing.

Go ahead, soon bearing half right up a grassy slope to a stile, then turn left to follow a left field edge and then a farm track. At a T-junction in front of the buildings at **Barlavington Farm**, turn left, still on a track which you should follow round to the right. Just short of the farmyard, go left through a gate into **Barlavington churchyard**. Skirt to the left of the church, leave the churchyard through the main gate and turn left along a lane.

After 70 yards, fork right along a house drive which feeds via a bridle gate into an enclosed path. After another 150 yards, cross a lane and climb the steps opposite to a stile. Continue along a

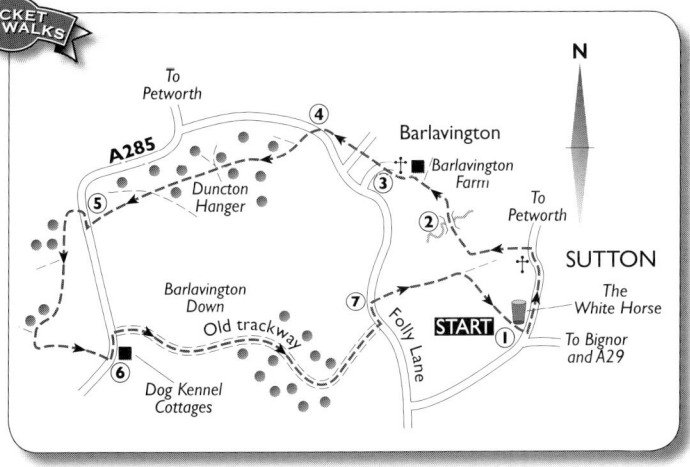

West Sussex

Taking a rest in Barlavington churchyard

right field edge and then straight ahead to a stile and across a field to join a lane over a stile a few yards to the left of a gate.

4. Cross the lane, go through a bridle gate opposite, set back from the road, and follow a path, fenced at first, then up through woodland. Where the path divides, fork right and, at a point where five ways meet, go straight ahead, climbing steadily through **Duncton Hanger** and disregarding a signed path off to the left. After leaving the wood, go ahead across a field, diverging at about 40 degrees from the right field edge, to reach the A285 and turn right.

5. After 60 yards, turn left along the drive to **Duncton Quarry**. After another 100 yards, just short of the gateway into the quarry area, turn left and immediately fork left along a path which runs within woodland, close to its left edge. Leave the wood and go

Sutton Walk 7

ahead, contouring along the hillside to reach another stile. Go ahead along a clear path until, after 150 yards, you can turn left along a chalk track and follow it out past farm buildings to rejoin the A285 at **Dog Kennel Cottages**.

Cross the road and turn left beside it, passing a row of cottages and a telephone box to enter a redundant loop of old main road. Just short of the point where this loop rejoins the main carriageway, turn right along a track between banks. After about half a mile, at a meeting of four ways, go ahead with the main track. Now follow this fine old highway down through woodland for over ½ mile, ignoring all side paths, to join **Folly Lane** and turn left.

After about 200 yards, turn right along a path which heads out, unfenced, across a large field. After a little over ¼ mile, fork right along a crossing path, also unfenced and staying within the same field. Go through a swing gate and squarely ahead across a garden to follow an enclosed path to another gate and on to join the road next to the White Horse.

Place of interest nearby

Bignor Roman Villa, within a couple of miles of Sutton, was discovered accidentally by a local farmer in 1811 while ploughing his fields. Subsequent excavation has revealed some of the best preserved Roman mosaics in England, including one over 70 ft long. All are on display under cover, open from 10 am to 5 pm between March and October except certain Mondays.
☎ *01798 869259*

# 8 **Fittleworth**

The Swan

The greensand heathland of West Sussex forms a fragmented patchwork of sandy commonland across the middle of the county, a carefully conserved habitat for some rare British reptiles which also offers superb walking opportunities. Starting beside the River Rother at Lower Fittleworth, this walk climbs out of the valley to traverse Hesworth and Fittleworth Commons, where the complex network of paths allows scope for extending the route within these delightful enclaves of heath and woodland.

THE PUB
The **Swan** is immediately identifiable from its wooden gantry and painted sign straddling the main road next to this 14th century pub, once a coaching inn. Inside, the low-beamed bar area is supplemented by a cosy restaurant and the distinctive Picture Room, adorned by the work of various

Fittleworth Walk 8

Distance – 4 miles.

OS Explorer 121 Arundel and Pulborough, and 134 Crawley and Horsham. GR 010184.
An undulating walk along good well-drained paths and tracks. One section of quiet lane.

Starting Point The Swan Inn at Lower Fittleworth. There is limited parking in front of the pub or alongside the B2138 as it approaches the river bridge to the south of the pub.

How to get there *From the A283, half way between Petworth and Pulborough, turn south along the B2138. The pub is on the right after about ½ mile and can also be approached via the B2138 from the A29 at Watersfield.*

artists. At the rear is a large walled beer garden. The beer on offer is Young's Bitter, supplemented by a regularly rotated guest ale. The lunchtime bar menu, of main interest to walkers, embraces the usual range of bar snacks such as sandwiches, baguettes and jacket potatoes with a generous choice of fillings, plus some more substantial dishes. Children and dogs are welcome.

Open from 10.30 am to 3 pm and 5 pm to 11 pm Monday to Saturday and 12 noon to 4 pm and 7 pm to 10.30 pm on Sunday. Food is served from 12 noon to 2.30 pm and 6.30 pm to 9 pm Monday to Saturday and from 12 noon to 3 pm and 7 pm to 9 pm on Sunday.
☎ *01798 865429*

Start the walk along a lane and subsequent access drive which leaves the **B2138** next to the **Swan** inn, passing in front of the

West Sussex

pub. Ignore the first signed path to the right. After about ¼ mile, turn right along a track into the wooded area of **Hesworth Common**. After a few yards, ignoring a left fork, continue with the main track, soon climbing gently within the right edge of the common. At a waypost, go straight ahead. At a second crossing path and waypost, once again go ahead. A short there-and-back detour to the left from this point takes you up to a fine viewpoint and a well-placed seat. Return the same way. Carry on, ignoring all side paths, to reach a road through a small car park.

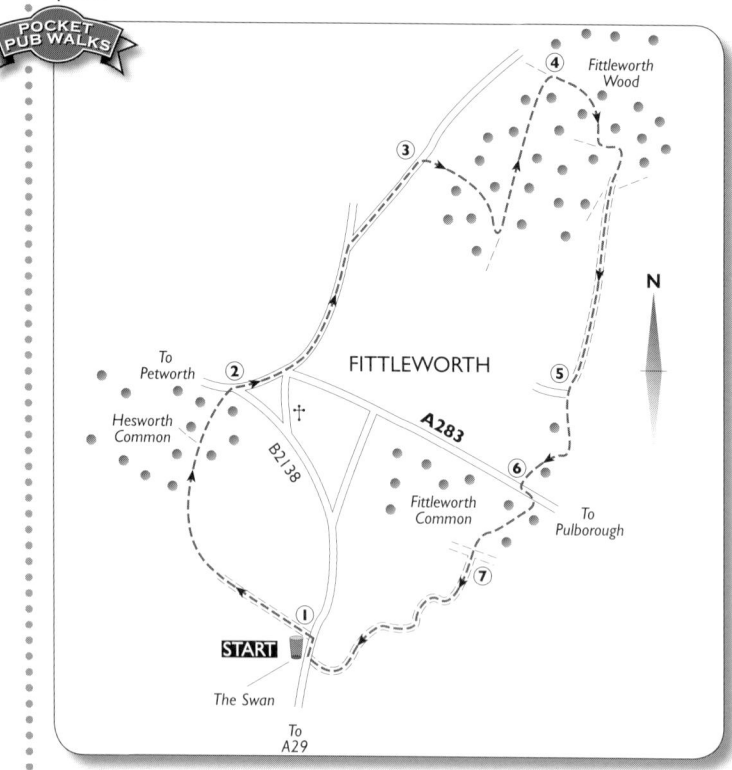

Fittleworth Walk 8

A shady path on Hesworth Common

Turn right and, after a few yards, fork left along another woodland path which passes to the left of a bowling green and a scout hut. Just short of a road, turn left along a path through to another road next to a junction with the A283. Join and cross the main road and turn right beside it, taking great care as you are on a dangerous narrow blind bend. After a few yards, fork left along a lane signposted to **Bedham**. Ignore the first left fork, continuing on the Bedham road.

After about 400 yards, just past the entrance to **Sorrels House** on your right, turn right along a signed path into **Fittleworth Wood**. At a junction with a wide track next to a cottage, turn sharply back to the left, climbing within the wood edge and ignoring all side paths.

Where the path levels out, turn right along a substantial crossing path. At a T-junction, bear left and, after less than 100 yards, at another T-junction, turn right along a wide path which heads generally southwards, within the left wood edge at first, then between tree-lined banks.

West Sussex

5) Where the track becomes a road and bears right next to a circular grain-storage container, go ahead on a path which soon climbs through woodland. Towards the top of the slope, turn sharply back to the right. After about 100 yards, turn left along an indistinct path within the left wood edge. Descend into a hollow, bear right and shortly fork left up to the **A283** road.

6) Ignoring the path opposite, turn left beside the road for about 60 yards and then go sharply right along an uphill path across the wooded **Fittleworth Common**. At the top of the slope, go ahead, ignoring a path to the right. Soon after passing under minor power lines, turn left, dropping fairly steeply down to join a lane and turn right.

7) After about 60 yards, turn left to a stile and drop down across a right field edge where a view opens out ahead across the **Rother Valley** to a wide swathe of the **South Downs**. In the field corner go over two stiles and turn right to follow the right field edge as it zigzags left, right and left again. Over another stile, turn right on a track along the valley out to the **B2138**. The pub is now a few yards to the right.

Place of interest nearby

About 5 miles to the east along the A283 is the **RSPB Pulborough Brooks Nature Reserve and Visitor Centre** where a 2-mile nature trail takes you across water meadows, passing several bird hides from which you can observe large numbers of birds, particularly in winter when controlled flooding is allowed to occur. The Visitor Centre is open from 9.30 am to 5 pm and the trail from sunrise to sunset.
☎ *01798 875851*

9 Ardingly

The Gardener's Arms

Much of this beautiful walk lies within High Wealden woodlands, rich in bluebells in early May. Starting from high ground, it quickly descends to cross a remote northern finger of the Ardingly Reservoir. After a steep climb it circles northwards, dropping down to cross the Ardingly Brook before climbing again to pass close to the main entrance to Wakehurst Place, where an optional extension of the walk for a tour of this 530-acre garden is easily practicable if time and energy allow (see Place of Interest box).

 The **Gardener's Arms** looks fairly modern from the outside but has a traditional low-beamed interior partly dating from the 17th century. The capacious bar and dining areas are made up of a number of interconnected rooms incorporating

West Sussex

Distance – 4¾ miles.

OS Explorer 135 Ashdown Forest. GR 342307.
A fairly hilly walk, mostly along good, but sometimes muddy, woodland paths.

Starting Point The Gardener's Arms on the B2028 road between Ardingly and Turners Hill and opposite the north entrance to the South of England Agricultural Showground. Parking, with permission, in the large pub car park or beside the road nearby.

How to get there Ardingly can be approached from Lingfield or East Grinstead to the north or Haywards Heath to the south. This is a walk to be avoided during major showground events as the approach roads become very congested.

two back-to-back inglenook fireplaces. It is a Hall and Woodhouse pub, offering Badger ales including First Gold and Tanglefoot as well as a regularly changed seasonal beer from the same brewery and a good wine list. The centrepiece of the large food menu is a choice of 'British Classics' and a complementary range of nationally inspired puddings. Sandwiches are also available. Outside there is a spacious patio and garden. Children and dogs are welcome.

Open from 11 am to 3 pm and 6 pm to 11 pm Monday to Friday, from 11 am to 11 pm on Saturday and from 12 noon to 10.30 pm on Sunday. Food is served from 12 noon to 2 pm and from 6.30 pm to 9 pm Monday to Friday, from 12 noon to 9.30 pm on Saturday and from 12 noon to 8 pm on Sunday
☎ *01444 892328*

Ardingly Walk 9

From the **Gardener's Arms**, turn right beside the B2028. After 100 yards, turn left along a signed footpath which starts along the drive to **Tillinghurst Farm**. Beyond a stile and gate, go ahead, passing to the right of a pond and farm buildings to reach another stile and gate before dropping down along the right edge of two fields and on, soon with the high perimeter fence of **Wakehurst Place Gardens** on your right. Go over a stile into woodland and follow the path left and then right across a long footbridge over a northern finger of **Ardingly Reservoir**. A path now winds up through more woodland to join a lane where you turn right. From this quiet lane views open out to the left across the next valley towards **Balcombe**.

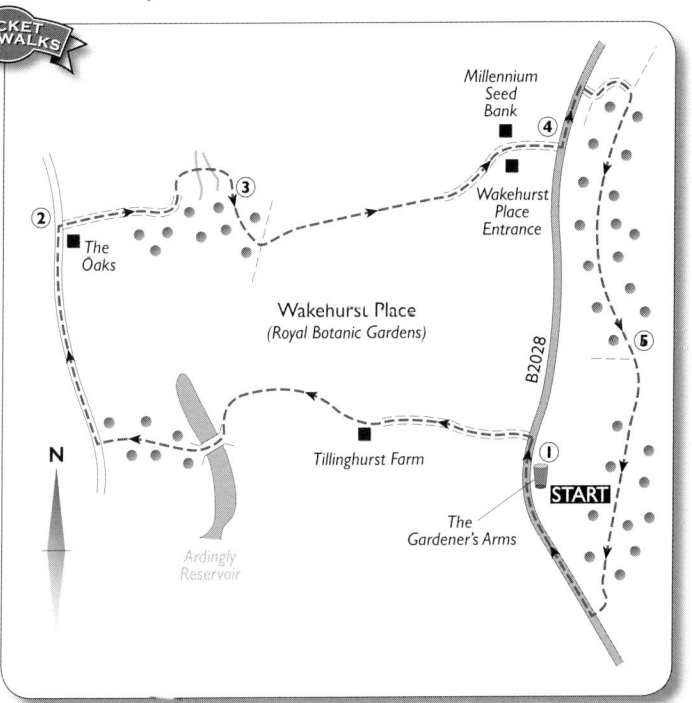

West Sussex

[2] After a little over ½ mile, soon after passing the entrance to a large house called **The Oaks** on the right, turn right over a stile and along a right field edge. In the bottom corner follow the field edge round to the left until, after 100 yards, you can go through a gate into woodland. Now bear right down through the wood to cross two footbridges, the second over the **Ardingly Brook**. Climb steeply, soon bearing right to cross a third footbridge over a side stream.

[3] Climb again where a wooden causeway has been provided over a boggy patch. Go through a swing gate in the **Wakehurst Gardens** perimeter fence, cross a gravel track and climb through ornamental woodland. At the top of the slope, go over a stile labelled **Havelock Farm** and follow a path between high deer fences where you may get a close glimpse of these relatively tame animals. Beyond the deer enclosures, go forward along a drive which takes you out past the buildings of the **Millennium**

Ardingly Reservoir

Ardingly Walk 9

Seed Bank on your left and the **Wakehurst Place** entrance building and car park on your right to reach the B2028.

Turn left beside the road where there is a useful path on the top of the grassy road bank. After 250 yards, turn right along a signed bridleway which starts between two cottages and drops down between high sandstone banks. At a T-junction, turn left and at another similar junction with a more solidly based track, turn right. Just short of a gateway, turn right on a clear path which follows part of the **High Weald Landscape Trail**, uphill at first, then along the side of a wooded valley where you will come across sandstone outcrops and some non-indigenous and fairly exotic trees, part of the original **Wakehurst** collection.

Where the path comes out into the open, ignoring a left fork, go ahead along the main track. Shortly, where this track hairpins right, go forward along a narrower path which continues along the hillside before entering woodland, gradually gaining height and eventually rejoining the B2028. Turn right for ¼ mile back to the pub and the start. There is a good grass verge or pavement all the way.

Place of interest nearby

Wakehurst Place Gardens, the main entrance to which is a short distance up the road from the pub and is also passed on the walk, is a country outpost of the Royal Botanic Garden at Kew and is a pleasant mix of walled and water gardens, woodlands and lakes. It contains important collections of rare and exotic plant and tree species from around the world. Nearby is the Millennium Seed Bank. The gardens are open daily from 10 am except on 24 and 25 December.
☎ 01444 894066

 ## 10 Staplefield

The Jolly Tanners

From the village of Staplefield where our featured pub faces on to the large picturesque village green and cricket ground, this walk heads northwards and eastwards, dipping through woodland at two points to cross small streams feeding south to form the headwaters of the River Ouse at the start of its journey to the sea at Newhaven. It then rises to traverse high pastures where distant views open up southwards towards the South Downs and northwards and eastwards across the wooded High Weald. The sloping terrain and well drained soil make this an excellent walk for the wetter winter months.

THE PUB **The Jolly Tanners** is a comfortable, friendly, independently run free house, with a bar area on two levels, one with an inglenook fire. The pub, regularly praised by the Campaign for Real Ale, prides itself on the quality and variety of its beers

Staplefield Walk 10

> **Distance** – 4½ miles.
>
> **OS Explorer** 134 Crawley and Horsham, and 135 Ashdown Forest. GR 274284.
> An easy walk, mostly firm underfoot, using good tracks, well drained field paths and quiet lanes.
>
> **Starting Point** The Jolly Tanners pub at Staplefield, next to the north-west corner of the village green.
>
> **How to get there** *Staplefield is 1 mile to the east of the A23 London-to-Brighton road, accessible via the main road exit at Pease Pottage, following the B2114 through Handcross. The A23 turn-off for Slaugham, further south, provides an alternative, direct, route.*

with up to seven on the go at any one time, the current choice being listed on the comprehensive pub website which also notes that, over the last two years, the pub has been able to offer 199 different beers from 88 breweries. The food menu has plenty of variety, embracing several pub favourites, regularly changed 'blackboard specials' and a particularly impressive choice of vegetarian dishes, including stuffed peppers and a stir-fried vegetable 'sizzler'. Children and dogs are equally welcome.

Open from 11 am to 3 pm and 5.30 pm to 11 pm Monday to Friday, all day Saturday and Sunday. Food is served from 12 noon to 2 pm and 6 pm to 8 pm Monday to Saturday and from 12 noon to 8.30 pm on Sunday, at least during the summer months.
☎ *01444 400335*

From the **Jolly Tanners** turn left beside the road with the village green on your right. Towards the end of the green, turn left along

West Sussex

a drive, leaving a telephone box on your left. Follow this drive for over ½ mile. After crossing a stream, go ahead, ignoring a left fork. After about 250 yards, fork right, still along a concrete drive.

2) After another 100 yards or so, go right up steps, through a wicket gate and forward along the left edge of two fields. After passing beneath power lines, go left through a gate, then ahead and subsequently right round two sides of a field. In the corner go left through a gate and forward, within the left edge of woodland at first, then obliquely down through the wood to cross a footbridge over a stream and climb.

3) At the top of the slope, leave the wood over a stile and go ahead along a right field edge, skirting to the left of the house and garden at **Jarrett's Farm**. In the field corner, cross a stile and go ahead along a drive, following it out to a road.

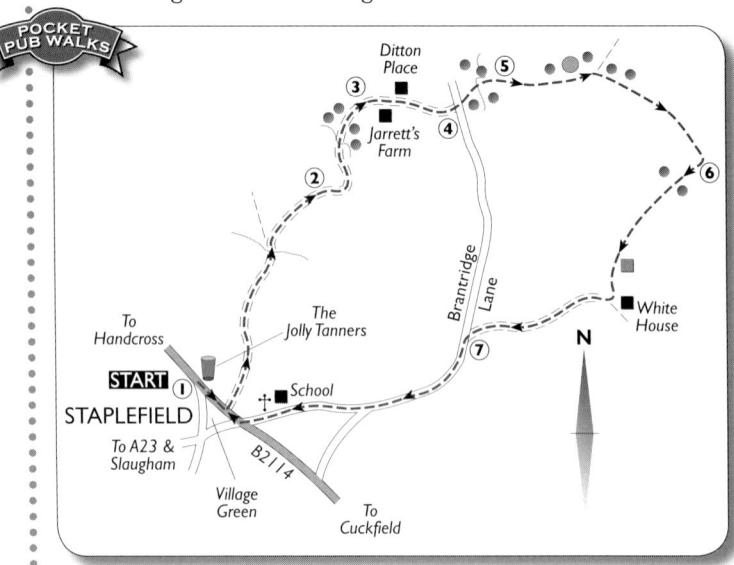

Staplefield Walk 10

A peaceful scene along the way

Turn left for 5 yards only, then go right over a stile and along a woodland path. On reaching a gravel drive, ignoring the path ahead, go left for 5 yards only, then right on another path which drops down through the wood to a stream crossing in a deep gully where steps and handrail provide assistance. On reaching a wide grassy path, turn left and, after a few yards, fork right to climb steadily up through the wood.

At the top of the hill, leave the trees over a stile and go ahead along the meandering left edge of several fields, crossing high, fairly level, ground with good views southwards across the heavily wooded weald to the distant **South Downs**. Ignoring a stile on your left, go ahead within a belt of trees, fringing the left field edge. Shortly go ahead over two stiles in quick succession, once more following a left field edge at first, then

West Sussex

straight ahead across a large field. Towards the other side of the field, at a broken stile, veer half right, still within the same field, passing to the right of a tree-shrouded pond and maintaining direction, aiming for the stile in sight.

[6] Over this stile, turn right along a gravel track for 30 yards and then go left along a woodland path, rather unusually laid with a line of paving stones (probably best avoided as they tend to be slippery). After leaving the trees, a path continues along the wood edge, rather unnecessarily hemmed in by a fence on your left. The path becomes a more substantial track which drops gently down, passing to the right of a large farm complex. At a T-junction with the access drive from a large house (**The White House**), turn right and follow it for ½ mile.

[7] Where the drive bends right, a few yards short of a lane, go ahead down a bank and steps to join the lane and turn left. At a road junction, keep right, signposted to **Staplefield**. Follow this lane for another ¼ mile, passing **Staplefield parish church and school** on the right, to reach a road junction at the corner of the village green. Turn right back to the start.

Place of interest nearby

A mile up the road from Staplefield, on the edge of Handcross, is **Nymans Garden**, now owned and managed by the National Trust. It contains an impressive collection of plants put together by the Messel family. Woodland walks have been laid out through a newly restored arboretum and down to an ornamental lake. The gardens are closed on Monday and Tuesday.

11 **The Haven** (nr. Billingshurst)

The Blue Ship

A**ptly named**, The Haven is as quiet and remote as anywhere in West Sussex. It is a tiny settlement, constituting little more than a handful of cottages, and has to be sought out in the midst of a thinly populated area in the upper valley of the River Arun between Billingshurst and Rudgwick. Like the circuit from Nuthurst (walk 12), this walk explores an intimate landscape of small woods and fields, staying generally level and dipping and climbing only to cross several small streams draining into the Arun, less than a mile away to the west.

The **Blue Ship** has a relatively modern exterior but inside, the main bar is something special. With low wood beams, an open fire and a brick floor, it dates back to the 16th century and, in company with only 200 other British pubs, has an

West Sussex

> **Distance** – 3 miles.
>
> **OS Explorer** 134 Crawley and Horsham. GR 084305.
> An easy, generally level walk, partly along bridleways which may be muddy in places.
>
> **Starting Point** The Blue Ship at The Haven. You may park in the pub car park with permission if also patronising the pub. Alternatively, roadside parking is possible nearby.

How to get there *The Haven can be approached either southwards from the A281 at Bucks Green or northwards from the A29 north of Billingshurst. At The Haven, follow a lane westwards, signposted to Oakhurst. The pub is on the right after ½ mile.*

honoured place in the Campaign for Real Ale's National Inventory of Historic Pub Interiors. It is a Hall and Woodhouse pub, offering King and Barnes Sussex Bitter and a regularly changed seasonal ale, drawn straight from the cask and delivered though a pair of serving hatches. The food menu embraces a choice of home-made dishes such as cottage pie or pork, apple and rosemary casserole. Vegetarians are catered for and the snack menu includes sandwiches, filled baguettes, jacket potatoes and ploughman's. At weekends when the pub gets very busy, you can spread out from the bar into three adjoining rooms or the attractive garden. Children and dogs are welcome.

Open from 11 am to 3 pm and 6 pm to 11 pm Monday to Saturday and from 12 noon to 3 pm and 7 pm to 10.30 pm on Sunday. Food is served from 12 noon to 2 pm daily and from 7 pm to 9 pm except on Sunday and Monday evening.
☎ *01403 822709*

The Haven (nr. Billinghurst) Walk 11

From the road junction next to the **Blue Ship**, start the walk along the lane signposted to **Garlands** and **Gibbons Mill**. On reaching a road junction, turn left through a gate and along a left field edge with a tree belt on your left. A few yards after this line of trees widens into a wood, go left through the remains of a gate and follow a clear path through **Smerrick's Copse** which descends to cross a stream and climbs again. Go half right across a wide grassy ride to follow the path opposite which continues through the wood. Shortly, at a signed path junction, fork right. On reaching another wide ride, bear right along it until, after about 100 yards, you can go left over a stile to join a lane. Turn right past **Heathers Farm** on your left.

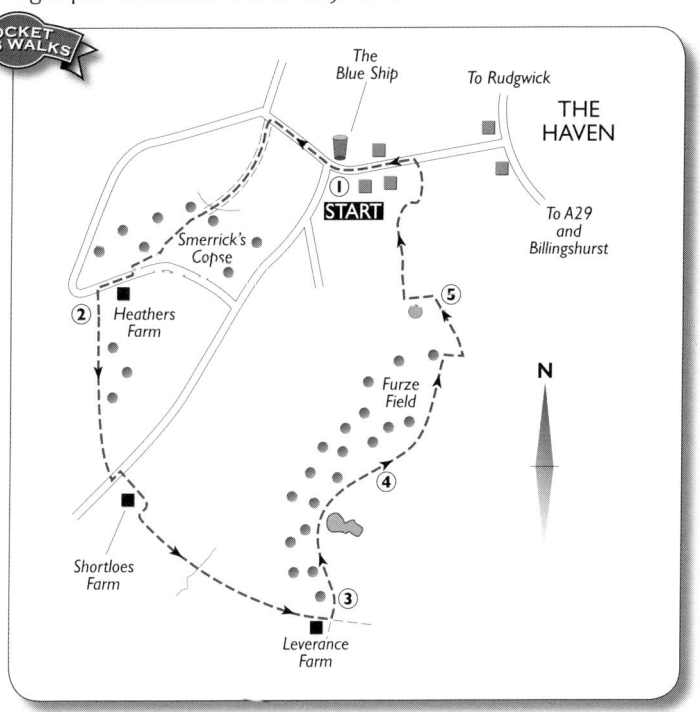

West Sussex

The pond passed at point 5 of the walk

2 After about 200 yards turn left along a heavily ridden bridleway which runs within a woodland strip, muddy underfoot in places. After a minor kink to left and right, the path, now with a much improved surface, continues through the wood to join a lane. Turn left and, after 20 yards, go right over a stile and forward along a right field edge. Follow this headland round to the right, around the back of the buildings at **Shortloes Farm** and then go left with a hedge on your right. The path enters woodland and dips to cross a sunken track and a stream using steps and a substantial footbridge. After leaving the wood, head squarely out on an unfenced grass strip across a large field.

3 In the field corner go left through a gap and along a gravel house entrance drive. After a few yards, join and bear left along an unmade access track which drops down, acquires a concrete

The Haven (nr. Billingshurst) Walk 11

surface and crosses an earth dam at the head of a large pond. At the point where the track veers left, turn right over a stile beside a gate and immediately left though a gap.

Now follow a meandering left field edge with a large wood on your left. After about 250 yards, go left over a shaky stile and follow a clear path through this old coppiced woodland, **Furze Field**. On the other side of the wood, cross a stile and go right for 60 yards. Just short of a plank bridge, not for you, turn sharply back to the left across the middle of a field.

In the field corner, after passing to the left of a small, nicely maintained pond, go left over a stile and ahead within the right edge of woodland. After less than 100 yards, go right along a tree-lined grass path. Where this opens out, sidestep to the right through a gap and turn left to resume your previous direction, now along a left field edge. In the field corner go through a gap and turn right to follow an enclosed path round two sides of a paddock and on beside a third paddock to join a lane. Turn left back to the start.

Place of interest nearby

At Newpond Common, north of Wisborough Green and accessible by road from The Haven via Billingshurst, is **Fisher's Farm Park**, a combination of farm and adventure park and a good place for a family outing, offering pony and tractor rides. It is promoted as an 'all-weather' venue with indoor play areas, and has a restaurant.
☎ *01403 700063*

12 Nuthurst

The Black Horse

West Sussex is said to be the most heavily wooded county in England. This record is not achieved as a result of large areas of afforestation but arises mainly thanks to an extensive patchwork of small areas of woodland like those encountered on this pleasant walk through alternating woods and fields to the south of Horsham. The pleasure of the walk is also greatly enhanced by the rich tree-lined hedgerows between almost every field.

THE PUB

The **Black Horse** occupies one end of a row of 17th century cottages originally built for workers on the nearby Sedgewick Park estate and has been in business for at least 150 years, probably longer. It is a free house in private ownership. The cosy main bar has an inglenook fire and leads into a restaurant at one end and a comfortable lounge bar at the other. The beers on offer are Fuller's London Pride and Harvey's Sussex Bitter,

Nuthurst Walk 12

Distance – 3 miles.

OS Explorer 134 Crawley and Horsham. GR 193263.
An easy, varied walk along field and woodland paths, mostly well established and signed. No significant hills.

Starting Point The Black Horse at Nuthurst. Patrons may park in the pub car park with prior permission. Roadside parking is possible near the church, just south of the pub.

How to get there *Nuthurst is signed southwards from the A281 at Monk's Gate south of Horsham or northwards from the A272 to the west of Cowfold.*

supplemented by a guest ale from a local Horsham Brewery, drawn straight from the cask and served through a hatch. The extensive menu embraces popular dishes such as sausage and mash or 'Pie of the Day'. Also available are 'light bites' such as filled baguettes or ciabattas.

Open from 12 noon to 3 pm and 6 pm to 11 pm Monday to Friday, 12 noon to 11 pm on Saturday and 12 noon to 10.30 pm on Sunday. Food is served from 12 noon to 2.30 pm and 6 pm to 9.30 pm Monday to Friday and all day Saturday and Sunday.
☎ *01403 891272*

[1] From the **Black Horse**, turn left along the road until you can go right, through the main entrance to **Nuthurst churchyard**. Pass to the left of the church to enter an enclosed path. Where this path ends, carry on across two fields of uneven rough pasture, bearing half left in the second field. Cross a stream in a wooded dip and continue on a headland track along the right edge of

West Sussex

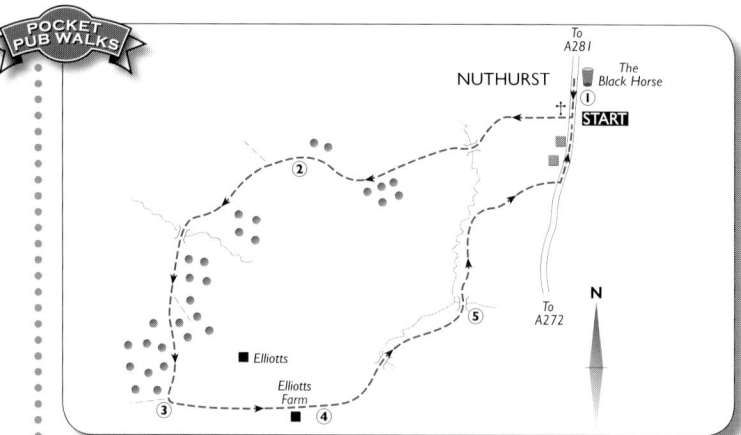

three fields, through a wood and on along the right edge of two more fields, still on a clear track.

2 Once through a wide gap into a third field, fork half left across a field bearing right along the far field edge with a wood on your left. At the corner of the wood, bear slightly left across the field to go over a stile into **Cripps Wood** in the field corner. Cross two footbridges in quick succession and continue on a path within the right wood edge. Where the path divides, keep right, within the right edge of coppiced woodland and then beside a belt of trees between two horse paddocks.

3 After another 200 yards, turn left along a signed bridleway which heads squarely out across two paddocks. Cross an access drive and go forward along the tarmac drive ahead with a large house in neo-colonial style, **Elliotts**, in view across the lawn to your left. Follow the drive as it passes to the right of a timber-framed and tile-hung cottage.

4 Where the main drive curves away to the left, go ahead on a wide grassy strip between more paddocks. Where this comes to

Nuthurst Walk 12

an end, cross a gallop and continue ahead along an enclosed path with a wood on your right. The path crosses a concrete bridge over a substantial stream and continues along the left edge of rough pasture. In the field corner go through a bridle gate and, after a few yards, keep left along a path, through woodland at first, then along the left edge of another field. A few yards short of the field corner, fork left, passing through another wooded strip and ignoring a signed path off to the right. Keep to the left edge of the next field, following it round to the left and down to a gate in the corner taking you back into woodland.

In Cripps Wood

Cross a culvert and, after a few yards, fork right to a bridle gate and bear left along a left field edge until you can go through another gate, passing back into woodland, now being actively coppiced. After leaving the wood once more, the path again follows a left field edge, taking you out to the road south of **Nuthurst**. Turn left back to the start.

Place of interest nearby

About 3 miles to the east of Nuthurst, via Monk's Gate, are **Leonardslee Gardens**, 240 acres of parkland and garden, offering a spectacular display of rhododendron and azalea in the spring as well as roaming deer and wallabies. There is also a restaurant and a display of Victorian motor cars. Open 1 April to 31 October from 9.30 am to 6 pm.
☎ *01403 891212*

13 Wineham

The Royal Oak

This walk samples the landscape of the Low Weald to the south of Horsham, passing through a pleasant mix of fields, mostly paddock or pasture punctuated by occasional small areas of woodland. The area is also notable for its many well preserved hedgerows, dotted with mature oak trees, sometimes shading small overgrown but picturesque ponds. Although relatively little used, the paths, part of a dense local network, are remarkably well signed and signposted, making it a particularly easy walk to follow.

Wineham Walk 13

Distance – 4 miles.

OS Explorer 134 Crawley and Horsham. GR 235205.
An easy, level walk along good paths and tracks.

Starting Point The Royal Oak at Wineham, where you can park in the large car park while on the walk if also patronising the pub. Ask permission first.

How to get there *Wineham is most easily accessible and is signed along a lane which heads southwards from the A272 about half way between Cowfold and Bolney. The pub is on the right after a little over 1 mile.*

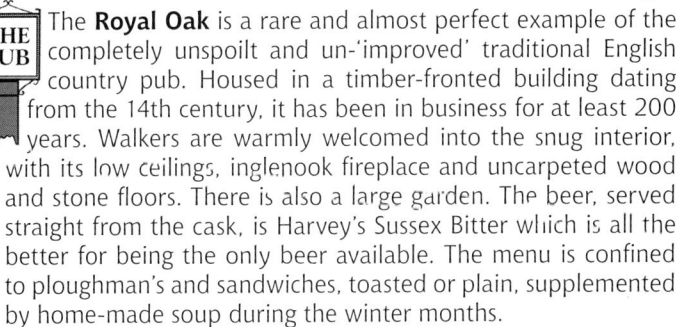

THE PUB The **Royal Oak** is a rare and almost perfect example of the completely unspoilt and un-'improved' traditional English country pub. Housed in a timber-fronted building dating from the 14th century, it has been in business for at least 200 years. Walkers are warmly welcomed into the snug interior, with its low ceilings, inglenook fireplace and uncarpeted wood and stone floors. There is also a large garden. The beer, served straight from the cask, is Harvey's Sussex Bitter which is all the better for being the only beer available. The menu is confined to ploughman's and sandwiches, toasted or plain, supplemented by home-made soup during the winter months.

Open from 11 am to 2.30 pm and 5.30 pm to 11 pm Monday to Friday, 11 am to 2.30 pm and 6 pm to 11 pm on Saturday and from 12 noon to 3 pm and 7 pm to 10.30 pm on Sunday. Food is served during opening hours.
☎ *01444 881252*

West Sussex

1. From the **Royal Oak**, turn right along the road. After 70 yards go right along a wide grass strip. Just short of a gate, turn right along a narrow path, soon ignoring a stile on your right. Where the narrow path ends at another stile, go forward along a right field edge. Soon after passing beneath power lines, sidestep to the right through a gap and resume your previous direction, now with a hedge on your left. In the field corner, go over a stile, follow a path through trees to a gate and then along a left field edge. In the first field corner, turn right, ignoring a stiled path to the left, still following the left field edge.

2. Just short of the next field corner, turn left over a stile, cross a drive and keep to the right edge of a garden, passing to the left of a shed to find another stile. Go forward with a hedge on your right, cross a stile in the field corner and veer slightly left to follow a path through a wood. Soon bear right along a wider track within the left wood edge, following it round to the left where another track joins from the right. After 60 yards turn right on a track which passes to the right of a gate and continues within a wooded strip.

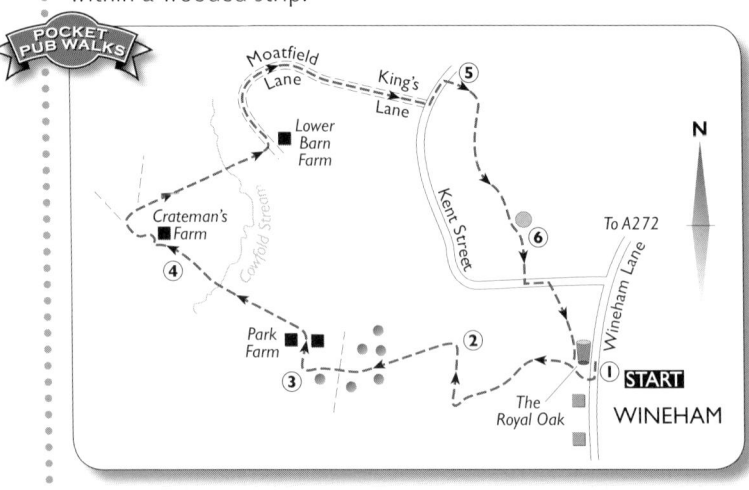

68

Wineham Walk 13

A tranquil spot on the return leg

Leave the wood through a bridle gate and turn right along a farm track. Pass between the buildings at **Park Farm**. Just short of the last barn on your left, go left through two gates and on along a left field edge. A trodden path continues to a culverted crossing of the **Cowfold Stream** and a gate. Now go ahead across a low-lying meadow, through a gap in a hedge and, in the same direction across the next field. Pass to the left of a cattle trough and continue with a high hedge on your right. In the field corner go left for 10 yards, then right through a narrow iron gate.

Now follow a signed path, forward for 40 yards, right for 50 yards, then left along the drive from **Crateman's Farm**, following it as it bends round to the right. After another 100 yards or so, turn right along a straight hedged path, signed as a bridleway. Where the enclosed path ends, go ahead across rough

West Sussex

pasture, re-cross the **Cowfold Stream** via a concrete bridge and maintain direction across a field to join a drive in front of **Lower Barn Farm**. Turn left to follow this drive, labelled on the map as **Moatfield Lane** and subsequently **King's Lane**, out to join a road. Turn left.

5. After 100 yards go right over a plank bridge and stile and ahead, passing a tennis court to follow a mown cross-field path. On the other side of the field, a few yards after joining a right-hand hedge, go right over a stile and sleeper bridge. Now head slightly right across pasture to a stile, in sight, and maintain direction across the next field to cross a footbridge and stile in the far right corner. Now bear left to enter a short tree-lined path which leads to a stile and then a path between hedge and post and rail fence. Where this ends, pass to the right of a large pond.

6. Just past the pond, side-step left through a thicket to a stile and then turn right along a right field edge to join a lane. Turn left and, after 100 yards, go right through a swing-gate and follow the left edge of two fields with a caravan park half hidden behind the trees on your left. In the second field corner, go over a stile and turn left, now back on your outgoing route. Follow it out to the road and turn left back to the pub.

14 Slindon

The Spur

As **the South Downs** decline southwards towards the coastal plain, they are folded into the gentle landscape of low rolling hills and quiet secluded valleys explored on this walk from the village of Slindon. It sets out across the fairly open farmed landscape of the National Trust-owned Slindon estate to reach the tiny hamlet of Madehurst. After a steep climb, the return leg of this fairly substantial walk lies within Rewell Wood where ancient yews jostle for position amidst a pleasant mixture of broadleaved trees and untended coppice.

The **Spur** was once known as the George Thomas Arms after the 18th century MP who lived in nearby Dale Park, traversed on our walk, and the original inn sign is still displayed on the

West Sussex

Distance – 5½ miles.

OS Explorer 121 Arundel and Pulborough. GR 970081.
A fairly strenuous walk with several ups and downs and one short steep climb. Mostly along good downland paths and tracks.

Starting Point The Spur pub at Slindon. Park in the loop of redundant old road in front of the pub.

How to get there *The pub can be found beside the A29 road to the east of the village of Slindon about 1 mile north of its junction with the A27 Arundel-to-Chichester road at Fontwell.*

pub wall. Although described as a coaching inn, the Spur has never really fitted that description. The 17th century building, sensitively modernised, now has a comfortable carpeted interior, incorporating a spacious bar and restaurant as well as a separate function room and skittle alley and a sheltered garden, well insulated from the main road. It is a free house offering three real ales on hand pump – at the time of writing, Greene King IPA, Courage Directors and Abbot Ale. The extensive and varied food menu, embracing popular pub food as well as more exotic offerings such as tiger prawn curry, is supplemented by a choice of snacks including sandwiches, filled baguettes and a variety of ploughman's. Children and dogs are welcome.

Open from 11 am to 3 pm and 6 pm to 11 pm Monday to Saturday and from 12 noon to 3 pm and 7 pm to 10.30 pm on Sunday. Food is served daily from 12 noon to 2 pm and 7pm to 9 pm.
☎ *01243 814216*

Slindon Walk 14

From the **Spur**, turn right along the nearside pavement beside the main road. After 150 yards, turn left to cross the road and follow a path which starts up steps and continues between fences, across a recreation ground and along a drive to join a lane at **Slindon**. Bear right, passing the thatched **post office** on the right.

Shortly turn right along **Mill Lane**. Where the lane bends right, go ahead along a wide track which climbs at first and then drops down through woodland. Ignoring a left fork, go ahead across a small open grassy area. At a four-armed finger post, fork left along a path which heads generally north, with trees to your left, for over ½ mile

Go over a stile, forward along an unmade track for 50 yards and then turn right along a tree-lined path. Go over a crossing track and the stile opposite to follow a well-trodden path with trees

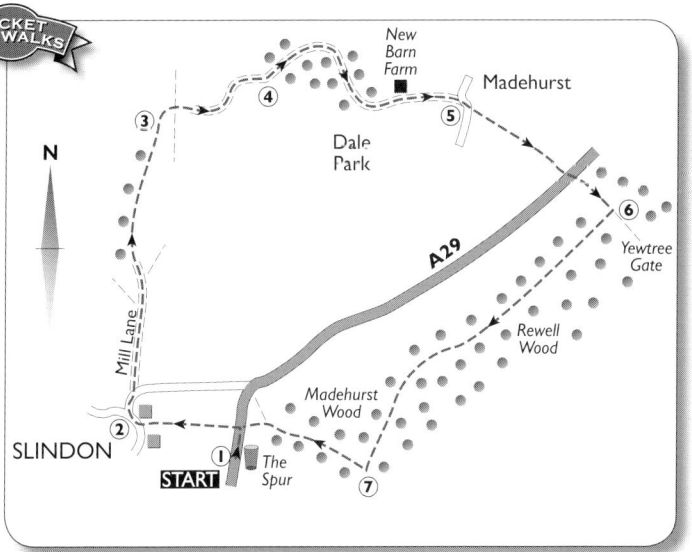

73

West Sussex

Striding out at point 2 of the walk

once again on your right. Pass though a dip and climb to enter woodland. After 50 yards, inside the wood, turn sharply left and shortly leave the wood over a stile. Cross the corner of a field to join and follow the left field edge as it curves right through another dip and up to a stile beside a gate in the top corner.

4. Over the stile, go left along a flint and gravel track. Join a tarmac drive on a corner and go ahead. At a T-junction turn right, still with the drive which passes to the right of a flint-walled cottage and drops down into a valley, part of the large **Dale Park** estate. At the bottom of the hill where a number of ways meet, go straight ahead, still with the main drive which begins to climb.

5. At a T-junction with a lane, turn right and, after 50 yards, fork left along a hard track, ignoring an immediate signed path to

Slindon Walk 14

the left. Disregard another left fork and shortly, where the drive ends, go ahead over a stile and drop down along the right edge of two fields. A path continues through another dip and up to join the A29. Cross the road and go straight ahead across grass to enter a path which climbs steeply through woodland, partly assisted by steps.

At the top of the hill, **Yewtree Gate** on the Explorer map, where the signed footpath goes ahead, turn right and, after 5 yards, fork left on a path which winds through the wood and soon follows a low earth bank, on your left at first and then on your right. At a meeting of five ways after 2/3 mile, go almost straight ahead along a path which starts immediately to the left of a waypost with the earth bank still on your right to begin with.

After another 2/3 mile, at a major waymarked junction, turn right along a wide path which drops steadily downhill. Ignore the first signed path to your left. When opposite the entrance gate into a camp site on your right, fork left along a path which soon leaves the wood over a stile and continues, stiled, across a paddock, through trees and across another meadow to join the A29. Turn left back to the pub.

Place of interest nearby

About 5 miles to the north-east of Slindon, via the A29 to Whiteways roundabout and then the B2139 to Houghton Bridge, is the **Amberley Working Museum**, a 36-acre open air collection of industrial exhibits, including a working narrow-gauge steam railway, vintage buses and regular specialised exhibitions during the summer months. A leaflet providing full details can be downloaded from the museum website (www.amberley museum.co.uk).
☎ *01798 831370*

15 Binsted

The Black Horse

Binsted is a modest settlement, comprising little more than a tiny isolated church, a handful of houses, a group of farms and a pub which has to be sought out along a quiet cul-de-sac. This walk, without significant ups and downs, explores an extensive area of partially neglected but always picturesque woodland to the west of Arundel. Being nicely sheltered, it is a walk which will provide protection equally from hot summer sun or cold winter winds. Make the most of this tranquil landscape as it may be irreparably damaged if a mooted new Arundel bypass for the A27 ever sees the light of day.

Binsted Walk 15

Distance – 4 miles.

OS Explorer 121 Arundel and Pulborough. GR 980064.
A generally level walk, mostly along good but sometimes muddy woodland paths.

Starting Point The Black Horse Inn at Binsted. You may use the car park with permission if also patronising the pub. Alternatively, roadside parking is possible nearby.

How to get there *Binsted is signposted southwards from the A27 about 1 mile west of Arundel, or from the B2132 Yapton road which also heads south from the A27.*

The pleasant but unexceptional exterior of the **Black Horse** does little to prepare one for the warm and welcoming interior with low ceilings, open fires and walls decorated with vintage posters and advertisements. A small bar for drinkers at the front leads into the main dining area and on into a conservatory at the rear, opening in turn on to a sheltered patio and garden, both overlooking an attractive green valley occupied by a golf course. This is a free house serving Courage Directors and Hopback Summer Lightning, but the emphasis is on good home-made food including a giant Yorkshire pudding filled with steak and mushrooms and a choice of regularly changed blackboard specials. Sandwiches and jacket potatoes are also available.

Open from 12 noon to 3 pm and 6 pm to 11 pm Monday to Saturday and from 12 noon to 6 pm on Sunday. Food is served from 12 noon to 5 pm on Sunday. The pub is closed on Sunday evening.
☎ *01243 551213*

West Sussex

[1] From the **Black Horse**, turn left along the road. Shortly, at a road junction, go ahead, signposted to **Arundel**. After about 100 yards, fork right along a tree-lined track, signed as a bridleway, **Old Scotland Lane**. It comes out into the open for a while, lined by young planted trees and then enters **Binsted Wood**. Ignore a signed path to the right and a crossing path. At a second signed crossing path fork right, indicated as a footpath. Descend to cross a footbridge and shortly bear right along the right edge of a cleared strip of woodland, following a clear path out to join a lane.

[2] Go left for a few yards and then right on a path on to **Tortington Common**, a mixture of woodland, patchy heath and scattered rhododendron bushes. Once over a sleeper bridge, bear slightly left, ignoring a path off to the right. Continue to cross another footbridge, on to join a lane and turn right.

[3] After about 100 yards, turn right again, over a stile beside a gate, back into the woodland of **Tortington Common**. The path stays fairly close to the southern edge of the common at first with occasional glimpses through the trees on your left across the coastal plain towards **Littlehampton**, then descending to cross a substantial footbridge. Ignoring a signed path to the left, continue along a wide path out to join **Binsted Lane** and turn

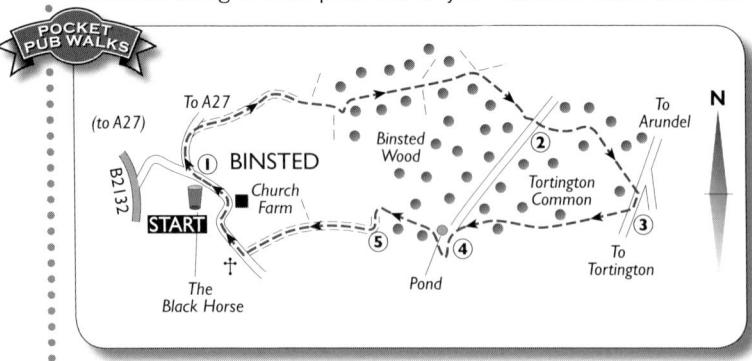

Binsted Walk 15

Binsted church

left. Shortly, where the lane loses its tarmac surface go ahead on what is now an unmade track, ignoring the first signed path to the right.

Immediately after passing a neglected but attractive pond on your right, turn sharply back to the right over a stile and along the other side of the pond, passing a rustic seat carved from a log and an unusually situated brick-built and ivy-covered wayside shrine containing a figure of the Madonna. Go forward through the wood to a T-junction of paths where you turn left. Shortly, at a crossing path, go straight ahead. After leaving the wood go forward along a right field edge, following it as it curves round to the left.

West Sussex

5. After about 100 yards turn right along a track which passes though another belt of woodland. Carry on, without change of direction, along a left field edge with a newly planted hedgerow on your left. From the field corner, go ahead along a hedged track which takes you out to rejoin **Binsted Lane** opposite the isolated **Binsted church**, of Norman origins. Turn right to follow this winding lane past **Church Farm** with its fine red-brick farmhouse, and back to the pub.

Place of interest nearby

The market town of **Arundel**, 2 miles to the east along the A27, is of great historic interest. The town is dominated by the castle, of Norman origin, but also has a fine old parish church dating from 1380 and a large Roman Catholic cathedral. **Arundel Park**, spreading out into the Downs behind the castle, is open to the public and offers superb walking opportunities.